This project was developed by Appleseed Press Book Press Book Publishers LLC

13 Digit ISBN: 978-1-60433-440-1
10 Digit ISBN: 1-60433-440-1

This book-plus kit may be ordered by mail from the publisher. Please include $5.95 for postage and handling.

Please support your local bookseller first!

Books published by Cider Mill Press Book Publishers are available at special discounts for bulk purchases in the United States by corporations, institutions, and other organizations. For more information, please contact the publisher.

Cider Mill Press Book Publishers LLC
12 Port Farm Road
Kennebunkport, Maine 04046

Visit us on the web!
www.cidermillpress.com

Design by Jessica Disbrow Talley

Printed in China

1 2 3 4 5 6 7 8 9 0
First Edition

PEANUTS CHRISTMAS COOKIE SET

CELEBRATE THE HOLIDAYS

WITH 50 RECIPES FROM THE PEANUTS GANG!

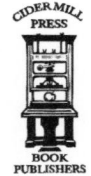

CIDER MILL PRESS

BOOK PUBLISHERS

KENNEBUNKPORT, MAINE

Artwork and Comic Strips by Charles M. Schulz

TABLE OF CONTENTS

INTRODUCTION

Nothing says holiday like the smell of cookies baking in your oven, and nothing brings the whole gang together faster than warm cookies and milk. This year, let the Peanuts gang join your holiday celebration with the Peanuts Christmas Cookie Kit. Kids will love the chance to use the enclosed cookie cutters to cut-out and decorate their own cookies, novice bakers will love the treasure trove of baking wisdom, and everyone will love the delicious cookie treats made with lots of fresh ingredients and a copious amount of love.

So this year don't forget about cookies for Santa, your mailman, your office party, and even your barista. You can wrap them, mail them, gift them, and yes, even eat a few during the few minutes you have between shopping trips, holiday parties, and reading classic Peanuts comics.

Are you ready to get started? Pick a recipe and let Charlie Brown, Snoopy, Woodstock, Lucy, Linus, Peppermint Patty, and the rest of the Gang be your guide to a yummy and jolly holiday.

BAKING TIPS FROM THE PEANUTS GANG

Baking great cookies is both an art and a science. Some people have the knack for throwing in a bit of this and a bit of that and coming up with a whole new concoction. Some people need to follow the recipe to the letter. Whichever kind of baker you are, these simple tips will keep you from saying too many "good griefs" and help ensure your cookies are the best they can be.

- It may sound obvious, but it is worth repeating: Use the best quality ingredients to produce the tastiest cookies. If it has been sitting around in your pantry for a few years, it might be better to throw it away and start fresh.

- Always use large-size eggs, unsalted butter, and pure extracts of vanilla or almonds. If you are planning on adding nuts to your recipe, use unsalted nuts too.

- Another obvious but critical tip: measure carefully. And watch out for the difference between teaspoons and tablespoons.

- Some products are easily mistaken for each other: Peppermint Patty once mistook salt for sugar when making a cookie recipe. Not even Snoopy would eat those cookies.

- Do not sift unless the recipe specifically says to do so. Instead, just lightly spoon flour into a dry measuring cup and level with a knife.

- Use either non-stick pans and cookie sheets or cookie sheets covered in parchment paper to ensure stick-free baking and easy clean-up.

- When you are cutting out cookies into shapes, be sure to chill the dough. You can soften it up at room temperature for a few minutes just before rolling it out.

- Leave at least two inches of space between cookies so they don't spread into each other.

- Adjust baking times to achieve the cookie texture you crave. A little less time produces chewier cookies; a little more time makes them crispy.

- Bake bar cookies in the pan size indicated in the recipe.

- Make sure the cookies are completely cool before you start decorating them or they will melt the icing.

TOOLS OF THE TRADE

The following is a list of utensils and kitchen tools that can make your baking life a lot easier. Lucy wouldn't bake anything without them. However, people have been making cookies for hundreds of years without any of this high tech stuff, so if you just have a mixing bowl, a spoon, an oven, and strong arms, you are still ready to bake perfect cookies for the whole gang.

ROLLING PIN

A non-stick rolling pin will make the cut-out cookies much easier to work with, but if you don't have one, to prevent the dough from sticking to your rolling pin, we recommend placing a large plastic food-grade storage bag on top of your lightly floured dough before rolling. This works great and makes things easier for the kids too.

ROLLING PAD

Along with your rolling pin, a rolling or baking mat will make rolling out your dough super easy. You can buy non-stick rolling mats, but many bakers say that just giving a quick spritz of non-stick cooking spray on a regular mat will do just as well.

ELECTRIC MIXER

If your muscles aren't as strong as Superman's, you might want to use an electric mixer (especially one of the big stand-alone kinds) to mix your cookie dough. Once all the flour and other mix-ins are in the dough, it can take a lot of strength to mix it on your own.

PARCHMENT PAPER

Talk about making clean up easy! Line your normal baking pans with a sheet of parchment paper and all you have to do is peel it off and toss it when you're done. Plus, your cookies will slide right off without you having to use a spatula to unstick them from the pan.

COOKIE PANS

Standard flat cookie sheets or baking sheets (or pans for the pan cookies) will work just fine for any recipe in this book.

BAKING WITH KIDS

If your children, grandkids, nieces, nephews, or neighbor kids are around, bring them into the kitchen will you for an afternoon of baking fun. To get the most out of cooking with the younger set, here are some helpful tips that with make working with Sally, Linus, and the rest of the little ones more enjoyable.

- The first step is always to wash everyone's hands thoroughly.

- Make sure clothes can get dirty or put on aprons.

- Use step stools (but make sure they are sturdy) to get the kids up to kitchen counter height.

- Read through the whole recipe before starting so you know what to expect. If there is more than one child involved, equally divide the steps so that everyone gets to do something fun.

- Pre-measure ingredients and let the kids pour them in.

- If the materials are soft, let the kids do the mixing. Anything with stiff butter or a lot of flour will be too heavy for their little arms to move.

- Expect a mess. Flour will end up on the floor, clothes will get dirty, and cookies that should look like Santa might look more like a big blob. That's all part of the fun of cooking with children.

- Have fun and don't rush the process. Sometimes it is more fun to roll out the dough than it is to bake it.

- Have the kids help with clean-up. Even a 5-year-old can help wash and dry the dishes. Putting things away is part of baking and kids need to learn this too.

THE RECIPES

SNOOPY APPROVED!

Here's a smorgasbord of more than 50 cookie recipes, some classic, some just a bit daring, and even a few meant only for decorating your favorite Christmas tree. No matter what you use them for, or whether you try one or try them all, these recipes are sure to be a hit with young and old, dogs and birds, teachers, friends, co-workers, and neighbors.

CUT-OUT COOKIE RECIPES

Use the enclosed cookie cutters or some of your own for these recipes:

THE PEANUTS GANG'S ULTIMATE SUGAR COOKIE CUT-OUTS

When the gang wants the softest, most delicious cut-out cookies possible, they turn right to this recipe, wash their hands, and start baking.

1 cup butter, softened
1 ½ cups confectioners' sugar
1 egg
1 ½ teaspoons vanilla extract
2 ½ cups self-rising flour

In a large bowl, cream butter and confectioners' sugar until light and fluffy. Beat in egg and vanilla. Gradually add flour. Divide dough in half. Cover and refrigerate for 2 hours or until easy to handle.

On a lightly-floured surface, roll out one portion of dough to $^3/_{16}$ inches thickness. Cut with floured cookie cutters. Place 2 inches apart on ungreased baking sheets. Bake at 375° F for 5-7 minutes or until set. Cool for 2 minutes before removing from pans to wire racks to cool completely. Repeat with remaining dough.

ADD YOUR OWN HOMEMADE FROSTING FOR AN EXTRA SPECIAL TOUCH.

2 ½ cups confectioners' sugar
¼ cup water
4 teaspoons meringue powder
¼ cup light corn syrup
Blue, red and yellow food coloring

In a small bowl, beat the confectioners' sugar, water, and meringue powder until combined. Use a mixer to beat on high for 4 minutes or until soft peaks form. Add corn syrup; beat 1 minute longer. Tint with the food coloring of your choice. Spread or pipe frosting on cookies. Let stand until set. Cover the frosting with damp paper towels or plastic wrap between uses.

LINUS'S CHOCOLATE SUGAR COOKIE CUT-OUTS

These yummy chocolate sugar cookies are a great choice for cutting out your favorite shapes, even if that shape is a blanket.

3 ounces unsweetened chocolate
1 cup butter
1 cup granulated sugar
1 large egg
1 teaspoon vanilla extract
2 cups all-purpose flour
1 teaspoon baking soda
$1/4$ teaspoon salt
Additional sugar

Microwave chocolate and margarine in large microwavable bowl on high 2 minutes or until margarine is melted. Stir until chocolate is completely melted. Stir 1 cup sugar into melted chocolate mixture until well blended. Stir in egg and vanilla until completely blended. Mix in flour, baking soda, and salt. Refrigerate 30 minutes. Heat oven to 375° F. Roll out to $1/4$ inches thick and cut with cookie cutters. Place 2 inches apart, on ungreased cookie sheets. (If flatter, crisper cookies are desired, flatten balls with bottom of drinking glass.) Bake 8-10 minutes or until set. Remove from cookie sheets to cool on wire. Decorate with icing and sprinkles.

For cookie pops, cut out the shapes as above, but before cooking, stick a lollypop-sized stick into the end of each one. Cook as above.

WOODSTOCK'S GINGERBREAD COOKIE HEROES

Woodstock likes to decorate these happy gingerbread men and women as firefighters, police officers, Soldiers, and ambulance workers and then take them over to a firehouse or police station to give a treat to his local heroes.

3 cups flour
1 ¹/₂ teaspoons baking powder
³/₄ teaspoon baking soda
¹/₄ teaspoon salt
1 tablespoon ground ginger
1 ³/₄ teaspoons ground cinnamon
¹/₄ teaspoon ground cloves
6 tablespoons unsalted butter
³/₄ cup dark brown sugar
1 large egg
¹/₂ cup molasses
2 teaspoons vanilla extract

Preheat oven to 375° F. Line cookie sheets with parchment paper. In a small bowl, whisk together flour, baking powder, baking soda, salt, ginger, cinnamon, and cloves until well blended and set aside. In a large mixing bowl beat butter, brown sugar, and egg on medium speed until well blended. Add the molasses and vanilla and continue to mix until well blended. Gradually stir in dry ingredients until dough is smooth.

Divide dough in half and wrap each half in plastic. Let stand at room temperature for at least 2 hours. Place half of the divided dough on a floured surface. Roll dough to a little over ¹/₄" thickness. Flour your work surface and rolling pin as needed to keep the dough from sticking. Cut out cookies with cookie cutters and place them 1 ¹/₂" apart on prepared cookie sheet. Bake one sheet of cookies at a time for 7-9 minutes. Do not over-bake. Cookies firm up after cooling. Remove cookie sheet from oven and allow the cookies to cool until firm enough to move to a wire rack. When the cookies are completely cooled, decorate your gingerbread men to look like your favorite hero.

SPIKE'S BISCOCHITOS CUT-OUT COOKIES

These traditional cookies of the southwest remind Spike of home even when he is visiting Snoopy for the holidays.

1 tablespoon ground cinnamon
1/4 cup granulated sugar
1 3/4 cups all-purpose flour
1/2 teaspoon baking powder
Pinch of salt
1/2 cup solid vegetable shortening
1/4 cup granulated sugar
1 large egg
2 tablespoons sweet white wine
1/2 teaspoon anise seed

Preheat oven to 350° F. Lightly grease cookie sheets or line with parchment paper. Combine 1/4 cup sugar and cinnamon; set aside. Sift together flour, baking powder, and salt; set aside. Cream shortening and sugar until fluffy. Add egg and beat well. Gradually add dry ingredients. Stir in wine and anise seed. Roll out dough between two pieces of wax paper until 1/4" thick. Carefully remove the top sheet of wax paper. Cut-out shapes and place on cookie sheets about 2 inches apart. Sprinkle the cinnamon/sugar mixture on top of cookies. Bake 15-20 minutes or until light brown. Transfer to wire racks to cool.

RED BARON
BUTTERGEBACK COOKIES

If you make these, even the Red Baron himself won't be able
to resist a fly-by to grab some.

3 eggs
1 ⅛ cup butter, softened
1 ⅛ cup sugar
2 ½ tablespoons vanilla sugar
2 ¼ cups flour
2 tablespoons condensed milk
1 egg yolk

Hard boil the 3 eggs in boiling water (about 10 minutes) and let cool. Peel the eggs and reserve the yolks. Discard egg whites. Beat the yolks with the butter, sugar, and vanilla sugar until creamy. Sift the flour and add to the butter mixture. Mix well. Wrap in plastic wrap and let chill in the refrigerator for 1 hour. Preheat oven to 350° F. Lightly grease a cookie sheet. Roll out dough on a floured board to ⅛" thick. Cut into desired shapes with cookie cutters and place cookies on cookie sheet. Mix the raw egg yolk with the condensed milk and brush the top of each cookie with this mixture. Bake for about 18 minutes or until lightly golden.

MARCY'S MOLASSES COOKIES

Marcy thinks these molasses cookies are "mmm, mmm, good!"

....

1 cup molasses
$^1\!/_2$ pound butter
2 teaspoons baking soda
1 cup sugar
$^1\!/_4$ cup hot water
4 cups flour
2 teaspoon salt
1-$^1\!/_2$ teaspoon ginger
$^1\!/_2$ teaspoon ground cloves
$^1\!/_2$ teaspoon allspice
2 teaspoons cinnamon

Heat the molasses to a boil. Remove from heat and add butter, stirring until melted. Place the sugar in a deep bowl and add soda to the hot water; pour water into the molasses. Pour the molasses mixture into the bowl of sugar and thoroughly mix. Add spices, flour and salt and mix with molasses and sugar. Pour into a loaf pan lined with parchment paper or waxed paper and refrigerate about an hour.

Preheat oven to 325. Cut dough as thin as possible and bake on a non-stick surface or a greased sheet for 15 minutes. Cool on a rack as soon as done.

Once you've made all the cut-out cookies you can stomach (and judging by the size of Snoopy's stomach, that would be a lot!), try these classic recipes. Every member of your gang is sure to find a favorite.

SALLY'S THUMBPRINT COOKIES

Sally makes a big indentation in the middle of these cookies with her thumb and then places her favorite jam or candy in the middle for a treat that is almost as sweet as she is.

2/3 cup unsalted butter, at room temperature
1/3 cup granulated sugar
2 large egg yolks
1 teaspoon vanilla extract
1/2 teaspoon salt
1 1/2 cups all-purpose flour
2 large egg whites
3/4 cup finely chopped walnuts
Hard candies or jam

Preheat oven to 350° F. Line baking sheets with parchment paper. In a large bowl, beat together butter and sugar until light and fluffy. Beat in egg yolks, vanilla extract, and salt. Gradually stir in flour. Form dough into 20 1-inch diameter balls. Dip in lightly beaten egg whites, then roll in nuts. Place 1 inch apart on prepared cookie sheets. Press down center of each with thumb to make a thumbprint. Place a small piece of hard candy or a bit of jam in each indentation. Bake for 16 to 18 minutes, or until golden brown. Cool on baking sheet for 5 minutes, then remove to a wire rack to cool completely.

Make these Thumbprint Cookies look even more festive by using either red or green glacé cherries (halved) in the middle.

LUCY'S PEANUT BUTTER CHOCOLATE "KISS" COOKIES

Even if Schroeder won't stop playing the piano and pucker up for Lucy, she can still give him a kiss when she brings over a batch of these irresistible cookies topped with a kiss of the chocolate kind.

1 ¾ cups all-purpose flour
½ teaspoon salt
1 teaspoon baking soda
½ cup butter, softened
½ cup white sugar
½ cup peanut butter
½ cup packed brown sugar
1 egg, beaten
1 teaspoon vanilla extract
2 tablespoons milk
Chocolate Kisses, unwrapped

Preheat oven to 375° F. Sift together the flour, salt, and baking soda in a small bowl and set aside. Cream together the butter, sugar, peanut butter, and brown sugar until it is fluffy and then beat in the egg, vanilla, and milk. When that mixture is blended, add the flour mixture and mix well. Shape into 32 1-inch balls and place each into an ungreased mini muffin pan. Bake for about 8 minutes.

Some people prefer to put their chocolate kisses right into the dough and bake them along with the cookies, while others prefer to press the chocolate kiss into the cookie after it comes out of the oven. Try it both ways and see which you like better.

SCHROEDER'S PINWHEEL COOKIES

No, Schroeder, you can't put these outside like a real pinwheel or throw them like a Frisbee, but eating them is probably entertainment enough.

1 ¼ cup butter
1 ½ cup confectioner's sugar
1 egg
3 cups flour
¼ teaspoon salt
¼ cup cocoa

Mix butter, sugar and egg. Stir in flour and salt. Divide dough in half. Stir ¼ cocoa into half the dough. Refrigerate one hour. On a floured pastry cloth, roll plain dough into a rectangle 16 x 19 inches. Roll chocolate dough the same size. Place on top. Roll out both types of dough until ³/₁₆ inch thick. Starting at the long edge, roll both types of dough together into a log. Wrap and chill for one hour or longer. Heat oven to 400° F. Slice into ¹/₈" slices. If dough crumbles while slicing, let it warm a bit. Place 1" apart on ungreased baking sheets. Bake about 8 minutes until set, but not brown. Remove from sheets immediately and cool on racks.

WOODSTOCK'S CLOUD COOKIES

These powder sugar covered cookies look fluffy enough
for Woodstock to fly right through!

1 cup butter
$\frac{1}{2}$ cup confectioners' sugar
$\frac{1}{4}$ teaspoon salt
1 teaspoon vanilla extract
2 $\frac{1}{4}$ cups all-purpose flour
1 cup chopped pecans
$\frac{1}{3}$ cup confectioners' sugar for decoration

Preheat oven to 350° F. Cream the butter with $\frac{1}{2}$ cup of the confectioners' sugar and the vanilla. Mix in the flour, nuts and salt. Roll about 1 tablespoon or so of dough into balls and place on an ungreased cookie sheet. Bake at 350° F for 15 minutes. Do not allow these cookies to get too brown. It's better to undercook them than to overcook them. While cookies are still hot roll them in confectioners' sugar. Once they have cooled roll them in confectioners' sugar once more.

ANYBODY HOME?

1-10-98

THAT'S A GOOD IDEA ... WHEN IT'S COLD, STAY IN YOUR IGLOO, AND BAKE CHOCOLATE CHIP COOKIES..

© 1997 United Feature Syndicate, Inc.

SCHULZ

IT'S AN OATMEAL-RAISIN COOKIE, CHARLIE BROWN!

Just like Charlie Brown himself, this recipe is a classic.

1 ½ cups all-purpose flour
½ teaspoon salt
½ teaspoon baking powder
¾ teaspoon ground cinnamon
¼ teaspoon ground nutmeg
2 sticks (1 cup) unsalted butter, softened
1 cup packed brown sugar
⅔ cup granulated sugar
2 eggs
3 cups old-fashioned rolled oats
1 ½ cups raisins

Heat oven to 350° F. Whisk the flour, salt, baking powder, nutmeg, and cinnamon together in a medium bowl. Set aside. With an electric mixer set on medium speed, beat the butter at medium speed until creamy. Add the sugars and beat until fluffy, about 3 minutes. Beat in the eggs one at a time. Turn the mixer to low speed. Add the dry ingredients and mix until just combined. Stir in the oats and raisins. Drop scoops of dough about 2 inches apart onto greased cookie sheet. Bake 15 to 18 minutes or until light brown. Check for doneness after 12 minutes, as oven temperatures vary.

Take this recipe one step further by adding chocolate chips into the mix for a super yummy oatmeal chocolate chip raisin surprise.

I THINK I'M ACTUALLY AFRAID TO BE HAPPY... EVERY TIME I'M HAPPY SOMETHING BAD HAPPENS

THAT'S NONSENSE, CHARLES...

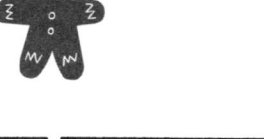
ANYWAY, HAVE A VERY MERRY CHRISTMAS..

NOW YOU DID IT!

PUMP UP THE JAM CHOCOLATE SUGAR COOKIES

Get the whole Gang dancing a happy dance with this chocolate and jam combo.

3 ounces unsweetened chocolate
1 cup butter
1 cup granulated sugar
1 large egg
1 teaspoon vanilla extract
2 cups all-purpose flour
1 teaspoon baking soda
¼ teaspoon salt
Finely chopped nuts

Microwave chocolate and margarine in large microwavable bowl on high 2 minutes or until margarine is melted. Stir until chocolate is completely melted. Stir 1 cup sugar into melted chocolate mixture until well blended. Stir in egg and vanilla until completely blended. Mix in flour, baking soda and salt. Refrigerate 30 minutes. Heat oven to 375° F. Roll small balls of dough in finely chopped nuts or sugar. Make indentation in each ball; fill center with strawberry jam. Bake 8-10 minutes or until set

PEPPERMINT PATTY'S PEANUT BUTTER BALLS

No peppermint here, but plenty of peanut butter goodness
makes Patty's day.

1 pound peanut butter
$1/2$ pound butter
1 and $1/2$ pounds powdered sugar
One 12-ounce package of
     semi-sweet chocolate chips
$1/4$ of one bar of paraffin wax
Toothpicks for dipping
Waxed paper

Place wax paper onto cookie sheets and set aside. Cream peanut butter and butter until combined. Add sugar a little at a time. Make sure it is mixed well. Roll peanut butter mixture into approximately 200 1-inch diameter balls. Insert one tooth pick into each small peanut butter ball. Set all of them aside. Melt chocolate and paraffin (parafin helps the chocolate become shiny when it cools) in a double boiler. Be careful not to over-heat the chocolate. Dip the ball into the chocolate so as to ALMOST cover the entire ball. Leave small portion of ball uncoated. Let cool on waxed paper. Store in a cool place.

This recipe can easily be halved if 200 cookies is too many. (Snoopy says 200 cookies seems just about right to him.)

YUM YUM BARS

If you ask any of the Peanuts Gang, they'll tell you these bars are their favorite no-baking-required treat.

....

³/₄ cup honey
1 cup peanut butter
1 cup semi-sweet chocolate chips
1 ¹/₂ cups mini marshmallows
3 cups rice krispies
1 cup salted peanuts

In a large saucepan over medium heat, melt together the honey and peanut butter and bring to a boil. Stir in chocolate chips and marshmallows, stirring until smooth. Add the cereal and peanuts. Blend well and remove from heat. Pour into a lightly greased 9x13 inch pan and pat firmly with spatula. Let cool slightly and cut into bars before hardening.

SNOOPY's CREAM COOKIES

One bite of these and Snoopy was ready to do his happy dance.

2 cup all-purpose flour
1 cup margarine or butter
1/3 cup heavy cream
Granulated sugar

Mix flour, margarine and cream into a dough and chill for an hour. Roll out half at a time to 1/8" thick and cut in 1 1/2" rounds. Carefully dip both sides of cookie in sugar and place on ungreased baking sheets lined with parchment paper. Poke with a fork 4 times and bake 7-9 min. at 375° F. When cool fill with filling and sandwich together.

CREAMY FILLING:

3/4 cup powdered sugar
1 teaspoon vanilla (or other flavoring such as almond or peppermint)
1/4 cup margarine or butter
Food coloring

Mix all filling ingredients until smooth, add a few drops of water if needed.

If making filling is just one too many steps, fill these with frosting, jelly, whipped cream, or even ice cream for a treat they will not soon forget.

PATTY'S PEPPERMINT COOKIES

Here are the peppermint cookies that make Patty do a flip!

1 cup granulated sugar
$^1/_2$ cup packed brown sugar
$^3/_4$ cup butter or margarine
2 large eggs
1 teaspoon vanilla extract
2 tablespoons water
3 cups all-purpose flour
1 teaspoon baking soda
$^1/_2$ teaspoon salt
6 ounces mints
Pecan halves

In a large bowl, cream sugars and butter or margarine. Add eggs, vanilla and water. Beat well. Mix flour, baking soda and salt well. Add gradually to egg mixture and chill dough overnight. Preheat oven to 375° degrees. Wrap each mint completely in cookie dough. Place 2" apart on lightly greased cookie sheets and put a nut half on top of each cookie. Bake 7-9 minutes until golden brown. Allow to cool thoroughly on wire racks.

What I did on my Christmas Vacation. I went outside and looked at the clouds.

They formed beautiful patterns with beautiful colors. I looked at them every morning and every evening.

Which is all I did on my Christmas Vacation.

And what's wrong with that?

SALLY'S SPECIAL KISSY COOKIES

Will Linus ever kiss Sally? Maybe not, but these cookies might help her get him to come over for a visit.

1 cup softened margarine
1 teaspoon vanilla
²/₃ cup sugar
1 ²/₃ cup flour
¹/₄ cup cocoa
1 bag (9 oz) chocolate kisses

Beat margarine, sugar and vanilla until creamy. In separate bowl, stir together flour and cocoa, blend into other mixture, mixing well. Refrigerate about 1 hour or until dough is easy to handle. Preheat oven to 350° F. Mold a tablespoon of dough around each kiss, covering it completely. Shape into balls and bake on a cookie sheet 10 or 12 minutes or until set. Cool, then roll in powdered sugar.

CRAZY CARAMEL CANDY BARS

Let's go crazy with the caramel candy bars. It's like adding a Halloween treat to your Christmas celebration.

1 (14 ounce) package caramel candies, unwrapped
1/3 cup milk
2 cups unbleached flour
2 cups quick-cooking or regular oats
1 1/2 cups packed brown sugar
1 teaspoon baking soda
1/2 teaspoon salt
1 large egg
1 cup margarine or butter, softened
1 (6 ounce) package semisweet chocolate chips
1 cup chopped walnuts or dry roasted peanuts

Pre-heat oven to 350° F. Grease a 13 x 9 x 2-inch baking pan. Heat candies and milk in 2-quart saucepan over low heat, stirring frequently, until smooth; remove from heat. Mix flour, oats, brown sugar, baking soda, salt and egg in large bowl. Stir in margarine with fork until mixture is crumbly. Press half of the crumbly mixture in pan. Bake 10 minutes. Sprinkle with chocolate chips and walnuts; drizzle with caramel mixture. Sprinkle remaining crumbly mixture over top. Bake until golden brown, 20 to 25 minutes. Cool 30 minutes. Loosen edges from sides of pan; cool completely. Cut into 2 x 1-inch bars.

IS THAT YOUR NOSE SNOOPY? BALLS

This quick no-bake snack kind of reminds the Gang of Snoopy's famous profile.

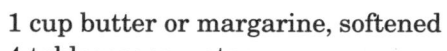

1 cup butter or margarine, softened
4 tablespoons water
1 teaspoon vanilla extract
6 tablespoons cocoa powder
1 ½ cup granulated sugar
4 cups quick-cooking oats
Powdered sugar
Flaked coconut
Chopped nuts

Cream butter with water and vanilla. Add sugar, cocoa, and oatmeal, and mix well. Roll into 1-inch balls. Add more water if necessary to make the dough stick together. Divide the balls in half. Roll half the balls in confectioner's sugar and coconut, then roll the other half in the chopped nuts. Refrigerate until serving.

IT'S THE
GREAT PUMPKIN BARS

What can we say? Linus insisted we add this recipe to the mix.

FOR THE BARS:

1 cup vegetable oil
4 large eggs
2 cups granulated sugar
2 cups canned pumpkin
1 teaspoon baking soda
1/2 teaspoon salt
2 teaspoon baking powder
2 teaspoon ground cinnamon
2 cups all-purpose flour

FOR THE FROSTING:

3 ounces cream cheese, softened
6 tablespoons margarine, softened
1 teaspoon milk
1 teaspoon vanilla extract
2 cups powdered sugar

Preheat oven to 350° F. In a large mixing bowl, beat together oil, eggs and sugar until mixture is creamy. Add remaining bar ingredients and mix well. Pour batter into an ungreased 15 x 10-inch jelly roll pan. Bake 20 to 25 minutes. Cool completely and frost with cream cheese frosting.

To make frosting, beat together all the frosting ingredients until creamy. Spread on cooled, uncut cookies. After frosting has set, cut into equal size bars.

Store any leftover bars, covered, in the refrigerator.

MARSHMALLOW CHOCOLATE BALLS

Lucy can make these on her own, with just a little help
from mom using the microwave.

1 cup of semi-sweet chocolate
2 teaspoons oil
1 (10-ounce) package marshmallows
Mini candy-coated chocolates
Sprinkles

Combine chocolate chips and oil in a microwave-safe bowl. Microwave on medium
setting for 60 to 90 seconds until chocolate is softened; stir until smooth. With
a candy dipping tool or toothpick, dip marshmallows into chocolate to cover
completely. Sprinkle with desired garnish; set on wax paper until firm.

Make these "balls of yum" match any color scheme by substituting the semi-
sweet chocolate with colorful melting chocolate found in any craft or baking
supply store.

CHRISTMAS EVE FUDGY FUN

Don't wait until Christmas Eve to get started making fudge. It's great for gifting to all the special people in your life.

3 cups sugar
³/₄ cup margarine
²/₃ cup evaporated milk
1 12-oz. package
    semi-sweet chocolate chips
1 7-oz. jar marshmallow creme
1 cup chopped nuts
1 teaspoon vanilla extract

Combine sugar, margarine and milk in heavy 2 ½ quart saucepan; bring to full rolling bail, stirring constantly. Continue boiling 5 minutes over medium heat, stirring. Remove from heat, stir in chocolate till melted. Add marshmallow creme, nuts & vanilla; beat until blended. Pour into greased 13 x 9-inch baking pan. Let cool and cut into 1-inch squares.

If the microwave is more your style, try this: Microwave margarine in 4-quart microwave-safe bowl on high (100%) 1 minute or until melted. Add sugar and milk; mix well. Microwave on high 5 minutes or until mixture begins to boil, stirring after 3 minutes. Mix well; scrape bowl. Continue microwaving on high 5 ½ minutes; stir after 3 minutes. Stir in chips until melted. Add remaining ingredients; mix well. Pour into greased 13 x 9-inch baking pan. Cool at room temperature; cut into squares.

TASTY TURKISH DELIGHT

If you've only ever heard about the delights of Turkish Delight,
now is your chance to try it for yourself.

3 cups granulated sugar
1 ½ cups water
3 tablespoons white corn syrup
3 envelopes unflavored gelatin
Juice of 1 lemon
³/₄ cup cornstarch
1 tablespoon of rose water (or vanilla)
³/₄ cup coarsely chopped pistachio nuts
Powdered sugar

Combine granulated sugar with water and corn syrup in a heavy saucepan and boil until it reaches 240° F on a candy thermometer or soft ball stage. Keep hot. In a small bowl, soften the gelatin in the lemon juice. Set aside. In another small bowl, dissolve the cornstarch in ½ cup of cold water, the pour it into the hot syrup. Stir gently and simmer slowly until very thick. Remove from heat, add gelatin and lemon juice and stir until gelatin dissolves. Stir in rose water or vanilla and nuts. Sprinkle a generous layer of powdered sugar in an 8-inch square pan. Pour in mixture and let set in a cool dry place (the refrigerator is too humid) for 3 or 4 hours or until set. Sprinkle with another layer of powdered sugar and cut into 1-inch squares. Dredge each square in powdered sugar. Store in an airtight container.

ADD COLOR FOR A CHRISTMAS COOKIE THEY'LL NEVER FORGET:

Additional ingredient: red or green food coloring

Add 2 to 3 drops of food coloring to the above recipe when you add in the vanilla and nuts.

ELF HAT COOKIES

These cookies have lots of different names, but at Christmas time
Snoopy just calls them "yummy!"

3 eggs
1 cup sugar
½ cup safflower oil
1 lemon, zested
1 orange zested
4 cups all purpose flour
2 teaspoons baking power
1 tablespoon lemon juice
Strawberry jam

Preheat an oven to 350° F. Whisk eggs, 1 cup sugar, oil, lemon zest, and orange zest together in a bowl and set aside. Sift flour and baking powder together in a large bowl. Stir in the egg mixture, kneading with hands until the dough comes together. Roll out dough to about ¼ inch in thickness on a lightly floured surface. Cut circles out using a cookie cutter or the rim of a drinking glass. Place a tablespoon of the strawberry jam in the center of the cookie. Pinch the edges firmly together to create a triangle, leaving the center open to expose the filling. Repeat with the remaining cookies. Bake in the preheated oven until golden brown, about 20 minutes. Cool in the pans for 10 minutes before removing to cool completely on a wire rack.

Add different fillings to the center of these cookies for even more great tastes. Try peanut butter and grape jelly, chocolate chips, apricot jam, and even a peanut butter cup in the center for a taste sensation Snoopy and Woodstock adore.

HE HAS THESE REINDEER, SEE, AND THEY FLY THROUGH THE AIR PULLING HIS SLED...

AND IF YOU BELIEVE THAT, I HAVE A GOLD BIRD NEST THAT I'LL SELL YOU FOR A DOLLAR!

HA HA HA HA!

MERRY CHRISTMAS, LITTLE FRIEND..

12-24

© 1987 United Feature Syndicate, Inc.

KING OF THE CLASSICS: CHOCOLATE CHIPPERS

When the smell of these cookies wafts through the house, even Schroeder will stop playing the piano and come by for a taste.

2 ¼ cups all-purpose flour
1 teaspoon baking soda
1 teaspoon salt
1 cup (2 sticks) butter, softened
¾ cup granulated sugar
¾ cup packed brown sugar
1 teaspoon vanilla extract
2 large eggs
2 cups (12-oz. pkg.)
    semi-sweet chocolate chips

Preheat oven to 375° F. Combine flour, baking soda, and salt in small bowl and set aside. Beat butter, granulated sugar, brown sugar and vanilla extract in large mixer bowl until creamy. Add eggs, one at a time, beating well after each addition. Gradually beat in flour mixture. Stir in chocolate chips. Drop by rounded tablespoon onto ungreased baking sheets. Bake for 9 to 11 minutes or until golden brown. Cool on baking sheets for 2 minutes; remove to wire racks to cool completely.

Pan Cookie Variation: Grease a 15 x 10-inch jelly-roll pan. Prepare dough as above. Spread into prepared pan. Bake for 20 to 25 minutes or until golden brown. Cool in pan on wire rack.

Slice and Bake Variation: Prepare dough as above. Divide in half; wrap each half in waxed paper. Refrigerate for 1 hour or until firm. Shape each half into a 15-inch log; re-wrap in wax paper. Refrigerate for 30 minutes. Preheat oven to 375° F. Cut into ½-inch-thick slices; place on ungreased baking sheets. Bake for 8 to 10 minutes or until golden brown. Cool on baking sheets for 2 minutes; remove to wire racks to cool completely.

Nutty Variation: Make them go nuts by adding walnuts, peanuts, or any other kind of nut that strikes your fancy to this recipe.

SNOOPY'S SNICKERDOODLE SURPRISE

Please Charlie Brown, please can you make these for Snoopy? Oh,
Woodstock wants some too? You'd better make a double batch.

¹/₂ cup butter, softened
1 cup plus 2 tablespoons sugar, divided
1 egg
¹/₂ teaspoon vanilla extract
1 ¹/₂ cups all-purpose flour
¹/₄ teaspoon baking soda
¹/₄ teaspoon cream of tartar
1 teaspoon ground cinnamon

In a large bowl, cream butter and 1 cup sugar until light and fluffy. Beat in egg
and vanilla. Combine the flour, baking soda and cream of tartar; gradually add
to the creamed mixture and mix well. In a small bowl, combine cinnamon and
remaining sugar. Shape dough into 1-in. balls; roll in cinnamon-sugar. Place 2
inches apart on ungreased baking sheets. Bake at 375° F for 10-12 minutes or
until lightly browned. Remove to wire racks to cool.

SNOOPY, WHO AM I KIDDING?

LUCY IS RIGHT..SANTA CLAUS IS NEVER GOING TO BRING A DOG TO SOMEONE WHOSE MOM DOESN'T WANT HIM TO HAVE A DOG..

IF I'M LUCKY, I'LL GET A PAIR OF SOCKS AND AN ORANGE..

IF I GET A RUBBER BONE, I'LL SHARE IT..

CHERRY ALMOND BISCOTTI

Wrap up these cookies with a pound of coffee for a gift
they will enjoy over and over again.

1 ¾ cups dried cherries
½ cup amaretto (almond-flavored liqueur), plus more if needed
3 cups all-purpose flour, plus more for work surface
2 teaspoons baking powder
½ teaspoon coarse salt
4 tablespoons (½ stick) unsalted butter, room temperature
1 cup granulated sugar
4 large eggs (3 whole, 1 lightly beaten)
2 teaspoons pure vanilla extract
¾ cup whole blanched almonds, chopped
3 tablespoons coarse sanding sugar

Preheat oven to 325° F. Heat cherries and liqueur in a small saucepan over medium-low heat, stirring occasionally, until cherries have softened, about 8 minutes. Drain, reserving 2 tablespoons liquid. If liquid equals less than 2 tablespoons, add enough liqueur to make 2 tablespoons. Sift together flour, baking powder, and salt into a bowl. Put butter and granulated sugar in the bowl of an electric mixer fitted with the paddle attachment; mix on medium speed until fluffy, about 2 minutes. Mix in 3 whole eggs, one at a time. Mix in reserved cherry liquid and the vanilla. Reduce speed to low, and gradually mix in flour mixture. Stir in cherries and almonds.

On a lightly floured surface, halve dough. Shape each half into a 12 ¹/₂ by 2 ¹/₂ inch log. Flatten logs to ¹/₂ inch thick. Transfer to a baking sheet lined with a parchment paper. Brush logs with beaten egg; sprinkle with the sanding sugar. Bake 35 minutes, rotating sheets halfway through. Transfer to wire racks to cool, about 20 minutes. Reduce oven temperature to 300° F.

Cut each log on the diagonal into 16 to 18 pieces. Transfer pieces to racks, laying them on sides. Set racks on baking sheets. Bake 8 minutes; flip. Bake 8 minutes more. Let cool until crisp. Cookies can be stored in an airtight container at room temperature up to 1 week.

CHOCOLATE COVERED COOKIES

Lucy requests that all patients bring some of these chocolate covered cookies when visiting her office during the holiday season.

¾ cup sugar
1 egg
½ cup butter, softened
1 teaspoon vanilla extract
1 cup all-purpose flour
⅓ cup baking cocoa
½ teaspoon baking soda
¼ teaspoon salt
½ cup chopped almonds
½ cup miniature semisweet chocolate chips
12 ounces white candy coating disks, melted
12 ounces dark chocolate candy coating disks, melted
2 ounces milk chocolate candy coating disks, melted

In a large bowl, cream butter and sugar. Beat in egg and vanilla. Combine the flour, cocoa, baking soda and salt; gradually add to the creamed mixture. Stir in almonds and chocolate chips. Cover and refrigerate for 2 hours. Divide dough in half. Shape into two 8-in. rolls; wrap each in plastic wrap. Refrigerate for 3 hours or until firm and then unwrap and cut into 1/4-in. slices. Place 2 in. apart on greased baking sheets. Bake at 350° F for 8-10 minutes or until set. Remove to wire racks to cool.

Dip half of the cookies in white coating; allow excess to drip off. Place on waxed paper. Repeat with remaining cookies in dark chocolate coating.

Place milk chocolate coating in a re-sealable plastic bag; cut a small hole in one corner of the bag. Pipe designs on cookies. Let stand for 30 minutes or until set.

Too complicated? Buy store bought cookies and just dip them in melted chocolate for a super decadent sweet treat.

CHOCOLATE AND PEANUT BUTTER: TWO GREAT TASTES SANDWICH COOKIES

Put these two tastes together to make a super special holiday taste sensation.

....

FOR COOKIES:

1 ½ cups all-purpose flour
½ cup cocoa powder
¾ teaspoon baking soda
½ teaspoon instant espresso powder
½ teaspoon salt
¾ cup (1 ½ sticks) unsalted butter,
        room temperature
1 ¼ cups granulated sugar
1 large egg
1 teaspoon vanilla extract

FOR FILLING:

½ cup unsalted butter, room temperature
½ cup homogenized creamy peanut butter*, room temperature
2 cups powdered sugar, sifted
Pinch of salt
2 tablespoons heavy cream, or more as needed
½ teaspoon vanilla extract
Chocolate sprinkles

Preheat oven to 375° F. Line a baking sheet with parchment paper. In a bowl, sift together flour, cocoa, espresso, salt, and baking soda. Set aside. In a large mixing bowl or the bowl of a stand mixer, beat together butter and sugar until light and fluffy, 2 to 3 minutes. Add egg and vanilla and beat until smooth. Add dry ingredients and mix until no traces of the dry ingredients remain, scraping the sides of the bowl to ensure that everything is fully incorporated. Using a small cookie scoop, drop dough by the tablespoonful onto parchment-lined baking sheets. Place cookie sheets in the freezer for 10 minutes, then flatten balls slightly with the ball of your hand. Bake for about 8 minutes or until cookies are just set in the middle. Let cool for 5 minutes on the baking sheet (they will deflate slightly), then transfer to a wire rack to cool completely.

In a large mixing bowl, beat butter and peanut butter together until fluffy and smooth, 2 to 3 minutes. Add powdered sugar, 1/2 cup at a time, mixing well after each addition. Add salt, cream, and vanilla and beat until smooth. At this point you may need to add more cream or more powdered sugar as needed to achieve the desired consistency.

To assemble, spread or pipe about 1 tablespoon of filling onto half of the cookies, then top with remaining cookies. Press lightly until filling spreads to edges.

Give these cookies a festive holiday flair by rolling the edges in red and green sprinkles.

FRIEDA'S CANDY BAR COOKIES

Frieda uses refrigerated cookie dough for these cookies so she has more time to care for her naturally curly hair.

....

$^1/_2$ tube refrigerated sugar cookie dough, softened
$^1/_4$ cup all-purpose flour
Snickers candy bars
Red and green colored sugar

In a small bowl, beat cookie dough and flour until combined. Shape 1 $^1/_2$ teaspoonfuls of dough around each candy bar. Roll in colored sugar. Place 2 in. apart on parchment paper-lined baking sheets. Bake at 350° F for 10-12 minutes or until edges are golden brown. Remove to wire racks.

For a sweet and salty treat, add pretzels to the mix.

LAYERED BUTTERSCOTCH BARS

Pigpen wants you to know that these are his favorite lunchbox snack.

¹/₂ cup butter or margarine
1 ¹/₂ cups graham cracker crumbs
1 14-oz. can sweetened condensed milk
1 cup butterscotch flavored chips
1 cup semi-sweet chocolate chips
1 ¹/₃ cups flaked coconut

Preheat oven to 350° F, (325° for glass dish). Line a 13x9-inch baking pan with a sheet of foil, making sure to cover the sites well. Place the butter in the baking pan and melt it in the oven. Sprinkle crumbs over butter; pour condensed milk evenly on top of crumbs. Top with remaining ingredients in order listed; press down firmly with fork. Bake 25 minutes or until lightly browned. Cool. Chill if desired. Cut into bars. Store covered at room temperature.

A HAYSTACK
FOR WOODSTOCK

Snoopy has his doghouse and Woodstock has his…haystack? Well,
he's willing to try it if you're willing to make it! No baking is required
for this yummy concoction.

2 cups semisweet chocolate chips
2 cups butterscotch chips
1 12-ounce can of cocktail peanuts
5 ounces chow-mein noodles

Melt chocolate and butterscotch chips in the top of a double boiler over hot (not boiling) water. Stir in nuts and noodles. Drop by teaspoonfuls onto waxed paper-lined cookie sheet. Cool. Store covered in the refrigerator.

FOR DECORATION ONLY

These 2 recipes are perfect for decorating around your house. Just watch out if you have dogs. Snoopy and his friends are a little less picky about what they will gobble down than the 2-legged animals in your home.

CHARLIE BROWN'S CHRISTMAS TREE COOKIES

When Charlie Brown is ready to decorate his little tree with homemade decorations, he turns to this recipe. Just tell Sally and the rest of the crew that these are just for decorating, not for eating!

1 cup ground cinnamon
4 tablespoons white glue
$3/4$ to 1 cup water

Mix cinnamon and glue. Gradually add the water. Stir until a ball of dough forms. Roll out with rolling pin $1/4$ inch thick and cut with cookie cutters. Poke a hole and let dry at room temperature for 1 to 2 days, turning over every 6-8 hours. If desired, decorate with icing. Hang with ribbon and enjoy the fragrance!

LUCY'S STAINED GLASS COOKIES

When baked, the candy center of this cookie melts, making it look like a stained glass window. Lucy wants you to know that you can eat these, but since the melted candy gets very hard, it's probably best to bake them just because they are as beautiful as she is.

....

²/₃ cup butter or margarine
1 cup granulated sugar
¹/₂ teaspoon vanilla extract
2 large eggs
3 cups all-purpose flour
2 teaspoons baking powder
¹/₂ teaspoon salt
¹/₃ cup milk
40 pieces of colored hard candy

Preheat oven to 350° F. Grease cookie sheets very well or line with parchment paper. In a large bowl, cream butter and sugar. Stir in vanilla and eggs. In another bowl, sift together flour, baking powder and salt; add to egg mixture alternately with milk. On a lightly floured surface, roll the dough ¹/₄ inch thick. Cut into ¹/₄- to ¹/₂-inch wide strips and, on a well-buttered baking sheet, form into window frames. Alternately, cut with graduated cookie cutters so that there is a hole in the middle of each cookie. Keeping the colors separate, place candy in plastic bags and crush into small bits. Place crushed candies inside window frames. Bake for six minutes, or until candy is just melted. Cool on baking sheet for 5 minutes, until candy is hard. Carefully lift cookies off baking sheet with spatula.

ABOUT
CIDER MILL PRESS

Good ideas ripen with time. From seed to harvest, Cider Mill Press brings fine reading, information, and entertainment together between the covers of its creatively crafted books. Our Cider Mill bears fruit twice a year, publishing a new crop of titles each spring and fall.

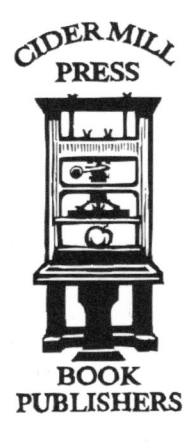

Visit us on the web at:
www.cidermillpress.com

Or write to us at:
12 Port Farm Road
Kennebunkport, Maine 04046